Dear Abba

Morning and Evening Prayer

BRENNAN MANNING

with JOHN BLASE

William B. Eerdmans Publishin
Grand Rapids, Michigan / Ca

© 2013 by Brennan Manning
This edition published 2014 by Wm. B. Eerdmans Publishing Co.
in association with the literary agency of Alive Communications, Inc.,
7680 Goddard Street, Suite 200, Colorado Springs, Colorado 80920
www.alivecommunications.com

Wm. B. Eerdmans Publishing Co.
2140 Oak Industrial Drive N.E., Grand Rapids, Michigan 49505 /
P.O. Box 163, Cambridge CB3 9PU U.K.
www.eerdmans.com

Printed in the United States of America

20 19 18 17 16 15 14   7 6 5 4 3 2 1

ISBN 978-0-8028-7199-2

The author and publisher wish to thank the publishers listed on pages 126-28
for permission to reprint material from their publications.

Dear Abba

Note

This collection of devotions is structurally based on the classic morning and evening approach used in The Book of Common Prayer. I have gathered three pieces for each entry, adhering to the promise of Matthew 18:20 — "where two or three gather in My name, there I am with them."

These devotions are intended for personal use. You can use them in a group setting if you choose, but that's not how I envisioned them. My prayer is these words will push you closer to that place of quiet rest, near to the heart of Abba, just the two of you.

Each entry concludes with a prayer. I've addressed them all to Abba, but you may have another name for God. Just remember: pray as you can, not as you can't. And if you call Jesus Goodness, he will be good to you; if you call him Love, he will be loving to you; but if you call him Compassion, he will know that you know.

Under the Mercy,
BRENNAN MANNING

Dear Abba

"But when the kindness and love of God our Savior appeared, he saved us, not because of righteous things we had done, but because of his mercy. He saved us through the washing of rebirth and renewal by the Holy Spirit, whom he poured out on us generously through Jesus Christ our Savior, so that, having been justified by his grace, we might become heirs having the hope of eternal life."

TITUS 3:4-7

To live in the wisdom of accepted tenderness is to let go of cares and concerns, to stop organizing means to ends and simply *be* in each moment of awareness as an end in itself. . . . We can embrace our whole life story in the knowledge that we have been graced and made beautiful by the providence of our past history. All the wrong turns in the past, the detours, mistakes, moral lapses, everything that is irrevocably ugly or painful, melts and dissolves in the warm glow of accepted tenderness. As theologian Kevin O'Shea writes, "One rejoices in being unfrightened to be open to the healing presence, no matter what one might be or what one might have done."

A Glimpse of Jesus

Dear Abba,

The voices in my head this morning are hounding me with the recurring moments I've turned away from You because I could not part with all my rich young ruler wealth, the numerous days I've Judas-kissed Your cheek in the garden of betrayal, and the countless times I've warmed myself by a traitor's fire and declared like Peter, "I do not know Him!" But then Your accepting voice scatters them all with a mercy fierce and ultimately kind, and I remember that I am loved. I want to simply *be* in You this day.

"Can a mother forget the baby at her breast and have no compassion on the child she has borne? Though she may forget,
I will not forget you! See, I have engraved you on the palms of
my hands; your walls are ever before me."

ISAIAH 49:15-16

Tenderness awakens within the security of knowing we are
thoroughly and sincerely liked by someone. The mere presence of that special someone in a crowded room brings an
inward sigh of relief and a strong sense of feeling safe. How
would you respond if I asked you this question: "Do you
honestly believe God *likes* you, not just loves you because
theologically God *has* to love you?" If you could answer with
gut-level honesty, "Oh, yes, my Abba is very fond of me,"
you would experience a serene compassion for yourself that
approximates the meaning of tenderness.

Abba's Child

Dear Abba,

I've come to the place where I'm letting You love me more each day, but I still struggle with letting You like me. I realize that has much more to do with me than with You, not to mention my ongoing cycle of attraction to tenderness, then repulsion, then back again. Thank You for Your still, small advances toward me displaying that yes, my Abba is very fond of me! Please help my unbelief. I want to rest safe in Your arms.

"At that time the disciples came to Jesus and asked, 'Who, then, is the greatest in the kingdom of heaven?' He called a little child to him, and placed the child among them. And he said: 'Truly I tell you, unless you change and become like little children, you will never enter the kingdom of heaven.'"

MATTHEW 18:1-3

For the disciple of Jesus, being like a child means accepting oneself as being of little account, unimportant. This understanding of ourselves changes not only the way we view our worth, but also the way we view God's saving grace. If a little Jewish child received a ten-cent allowance from her father at the end of the week, she did not regard it as payment for sweeping the house, doing the dishes, and baking the bread. It was a wholly unmerited gift, a gesture of her father's absolute liberality.

The Importance of Being Foolish

Dear Abba,

Your liberal gift of grace stands in stark con-
trast to this world's economy of work and
wage. It's much more than the difference
between black and white; it's like the difference between apples and engine blocks.
I want to start this day with an awareness
of Your absolute liberality. As the day rolls
on and I regrettably slip back into trying
to earn Your favor, forgive me, I pray, and
gently remind me that I am the child and
You are the Father, and it is Your kingdom I
desire — not mine.

"Now he had to go through Samaria. So he came to a town in Samaria called Sychar, near the plot of ground Jacob had given to his son Joseph. Jacob's well was there, and Jesus, tired as he was from the journey, sat down by the well. It was about noon."

JOHN 4:4-6

Instead of a mindless drifting through the insignificant, apparently superficial and nonreligious events of the day, our passive union with Christ can be made active by creative acts of the will, intelligence and imagination. How? By studying the life experiences of Jesus and relating them to our own; by poring over the Gospels and seeing the different scenarios not as historical events but as contemporaneous happenings reproducing themselves in our daily experience. Do we feel dry, weary, filled with a sense of failure? In the twinkle of an eye we can relate our mood to Jesus Who one day felt the same way and collapsed exhausted by a well in Samaria. I can invite this tired Jesus into my very discouragement: "Jesus, here I am, whipped, wiped out, in the pits, and all Yours."

The Relentless Tenderness of Jesus

Dear Abba,

I feel like I've had to go through Samaria a dozen times today. I'm tired from too many trips to town, each time greeted by thirsty and hungry people, veritable Humpty-Dumptys who've fallen off the wall and want me to round up horses and men and put them back together again. But I had to walk away; I just could not give any more. So Jesus, here I am, and this is certainly not a nursery rhyme. I'm wiped out — somewhere beyond the pits — but I'm all Yours, and I believe You understand.

"For it is by grace you have been saved, through faith — and this is not from yourselves, it is the gift of God — not by works, so that no one can boast. For we are God's handiwork, created in Christ Jesus to do good works, which God prepared in advance for us to do."

EPHESIANS 2:8-10

If a random sample of one thousand American Christians were taken today, the majority would define faith as belief in the existence of God. In earlier times it did not take faith to believe that God existed — almost everybody took that for granted. Rather, faith had to do with one's relationship to God — whether one trusted in God. The difference between faith as "belief in something that may or may not exist" and faith as "trusting in God" is enormous. The first is a matter of the head, the second a matter of the heart. The first can leave us unchanged, the second intrinsically brings change.

The Ragamuffin Gospel

Dear Abba,

Trust. That's what it comes down to, doesn't it? Putting all my eggs in Your basket, the one that says I am accepted and loved beyond measure even if I'm inadequate, insecure, mistaken, or potbellied. Even if death, panic, depression, and disillusionment are as close to me as my own breath, trusting You means that I am not those things, that I am something more than those things. Faith means believing that I am Yours and You are mine, that I am who You say I am: Your beloved, fearfully and wonderfully accepted.

"Jesus spoke to them again in parables, saying: 'The kingdom of heaven is like a king who prepared a wedding banquet for his son. He sent his servants to those who had been invited to the banquet to tell them to come, but they refused to come. Then he sent some more servants and said, "Tell those who have been invited that I have prepared my dinner: My oxen and fattened cattle have been butchered, and everything is ready. Come to the wedding banquet.""

MATTHEW 22:1-4

In Matthew 22, Jesus described the Kingdom of God as a wedding feast. Do you really trust that you are going to a wedding feast that has already begun? Do you really believe that God loves you unconditionally and as you are? Are you committed to the idea that the nature of the world is to be a celebration? If you are, then in the words of Father John Powell, S.J., "Please notify your face."

Souvenirs of Solitude

Dear Abba,

I don't have to loiter around the door waiting for the muscle to look the other way so I can sneak in. I don't have to pay scalpers' prices for decent seats either. And I don't have to wash cars or sell cookies in order to gain entrance to the party. I am Your child and I've been personally invited to the celebration; there's even a place prepared for me with my nametag and everything. Forgive my doom and gloom. Restore the joy of my salvation to myself, to all of me, starting with my face.

Fourth Day   *Morning*

"Since, then, you have been raised with Christ, set your hearts
on things above, where Christ is, seated at the right hand of
God. Set your minds on things above, not on earthly things.
For you died, and your life is now hidden with Christ in God.
When Christ, who is your life, appears, then you also will
appear with him in glory."

COLOSSIANS 3:1-4

In my first-ever experience of being loved for nothing I had
done or could do, I moved back and forth between mild
ecstasy, silent wonder, and hushed trembling. The aura might
be best described as "bright darkness." The moment lingered
on in a timeless now, until without warning I felt a hand
grip my heart. It was abrupt and startling. The awareness of
being loved was no longer tender and comforting. The love
of Christ, the crucified Son of God, took on the wild fury of a
sudden spring storm. Like a dam bursting, a spasm of convul-
sive crying erupted from the depths of my soul. *Jesus died on
the cross for me.*

Above All

Dear Abba,

The ten thousand things are already vying for my attention. Wait, actually make that ten thousand and one. Some of them are shallow — like what shoes I will wear today — but some of them are legitimate: lunch with a friend, a doctor's appointment, responding to a letter. Still, they are all earthly things. So startle me, I pray. Burst into the compound of my senses and steal me away from the urgent tyrannies already seeking to keep my eyes fixed on things below. You died for me. For me. That is the one thing; nothing else compares.

" 'I was ashamed and humiliated because I bore the disgrace of my youth.' 'Is not Ephraim my dear son, the child in whom I delight? Though I often speak against him, I still remember him. Therefore my heart yearns for him; I have great compassion for him,' declares the Lord."

JEREMIAH 31:19-20

The Greek verb *splangchnizomai* is usually translated "to be moved with compassion." But its etymological meaning is more profound and powerful. The verb is derived from the noun *splangchna,* which means "intestines, bowels, entrails," that is to say, the inward parts from which the strongest emotions arise. In American argot we would call it a gut reaction. That is why English translations resort to active expressions like "he was *moved* with pity" or "his heart *went out* to them." But even these verbs do not capture the deep physical flavor of the Greek word for compassion. . . . His heart was torn, His gut wrenched, the most vulnerable part of His being laid bare.

Lion & Lamb

Dear Abba,

I'm afraid far too many of my moments
of compassion are nothing more than the
warm fuzzies, experiences I can manage
and keep at a safe arm's length. These
illusions of compassion can fool my friends
and neighbors, but not You. When I consider this day, I don't know if my heart was
torn up about anything, my gut wrenched
by another's pain, or the deepest parts of
me hurled to the surface for all to see. I
know it's a dangerous request to make, but
teach me compassion so that others might
take notice and be drawn to Your beautiful
heart.

"But whenever anyone turns to the Lord, the veil is taken away. Now the Lord is the Spirit, and where the Spirit of the Lord is, there is freedom. And we all, who with unveiled faces contemplate the Lord's glory, are being transformed into his image with ever-increasing glory, which comes from the Lord, who is the Spirit."

2 CORINTHIANS 3:16-18

The tragedy of our attempts to compel others to be virtuous by force or subtle manipulation is that these efforts are so prevalent in our lives, so characteristic of our relationships with others that most of us, most of the time, are unaware of the problem. We do not perceive that we betray a basic lack of respect for the humanity of those with whom we deal, and that this lack of respect is the essential problem with the use of authority in the Church and in the home. If we really knew the God of Jesus, we would stop trying to control and manipulate others "for their own good," knowing full well that this is not how God works among His people.

The Signature of Jesus

Dear Abba,

I'm stepping into a new day brimming with
new mercies, fresh-slate-do-over grace
extended freely to me by Your hands. But it
is not just given to me but to all. So that my
attempts to control and manipulate others, even if it's in their best interests, is not
only to spit on the grace given them, but
also that given to me. Father, the only thing
truly "for our own good" is Your mercy.
Nothing else comes close. Nothing. Have
mercy on me.

"But if we walk in the light, as he is in the light, we have fellowship with one another, and the blood of Jesus, his Son, purifies us from all sin. If we claim to be without sin, we deceive ourselves and the truth is not in us. If we confess our sins, he is faithful and just and will forgive us our sins and purify us from all unrighteousness. If we claim we have not sinned, we make him out to be a liar and his word is not in us."

1 JOHN 1:7-10

Impostors in the Spirit always prefer appearances to reality. Rationalization begins with a look in the mirror. We don't like the sight of ourselves as we really are, so we try cosmetics, makeup, the right light, and the proper accessories to develop an acceptable image of ourselves. We rely on the stylish disguise that has made us look good or at least look away from our true self. Self-deception mortgages our sinfulness and prevents us from seeing ourselves as we really are — ragamuffins.

The Ragamuffin Gospel

Dear Abba,

To spiritually photoshop, or not to spiritually photoshop: that is a recurring question.
I've gotten pretty good at cropping and
resizing to keep an impressive façade, but
the emptiness behind it is the telling thing,
telling me that something about the life I'm
living is off the tracks. I'm not the biggest
fan of mirrors but I realize they do serve a
purpose: showing me the reality, the real
me. I'm a ragamuffin, always have been, and
yet You love me, the real me. Amazing.

"I have become its servant by the commission God gave me to present to you the word of God in its fullness — the mystery that has been kept hidden for ages and generations, but is now disclosed to the Lord's people. To them God has chosen to make known among the Gentiles the glorious riches of this mystery, which is Christ in you, the hope of glory."

COLOSSIANS 1:25-27

And yet it may happen in these most desperate trials of our human existence that beyond any rational explanation, we may feel a nail-scarred Hand clutching ours. We are able, as Etty Hillesun, the Dutch Jewess who died in Auschwitz on November 30, 1943, wrote, "to safeguard that little piece of God in ourselves" and not give way to despair. We make it through the night and darkness gives way to the light of morning. The tragedy radically alters the direction of our lives, but in our vulnerability and defenselessness we experience the power of Jesus in His present risenness.

Abba's Child

Dear Abba,

Even though the darkness has surrendered
to the light of morning the desperation remains, a residue from yesterday's tests and
trials and tribulations. I've tried to shake it
but I can't. There seems only a little piece of
You in me right now, maybe no more than
loaves and fish. Multiply Your power in me,
I pray. Feed the multitudes in me hungry
for something more than bread alone. I'm
holding on by my fingertips. I do not want
to give way to despair. You are my hope of
glory. You are my only hope.

"I keep asking that the God of our Lord Jesus Christ, the glorious Father, may give you the Spirit of wisdom and revelation, so that you may know him better. I pray that the eyes of your heart may be enlightened in order that you may know the hope to which he has called you, the riches of his glorious inheritance in his holy people. . . ."

EPHESIANS 1:17-18

The challenge, so keenly put in the New Testament, "Who do you say that I am?" is addressed to each of us. Who is the Jesus of your own interiority? Describe the Christ that you have personally encountered on the grounds of your own self. Only a superficial stereotyped answer can be forthcoming if we have not developed a personal relationship with Jesus. We can only repeat and reproduce pious turns of speech that others have spoken or wave a catechism under children's noses if we have not gained some partial insight, some small perception, of the inexhaustible riches of the mystery of who is Jesus Christ.

Souvenirs of Solitude

Dear Abba,

I have had glimpses of enlightenment,
quicksilver encounters that have allowed
me to say a little more of who You are. But
they've just been the tip of the iceberg.
Give me the eyes to not merely notice but
see. Give me the ears to not only hear but
listen. Give me the courage to further touch
Your scars. I want to taste more and digest
more of the riches of the mystery that is
You. Help me come to my senses and know
You better.

"It is for freedom that Christ has set us free. Stand firm, then, and do not let yourselves be burdened again by a yoke of slavery. Mark my words! I, Paul, tell you that if you let yourselves be circumcised, Christ will be of no value to you at all. Again I declare to every man who lets himself be circumcised that he is obligated to obey the whole law."

GALATIANS 5:1-3

In order to be free to be faithful to this sacred Man and His dream, to others and ourselves, we must be liberated from the damnable imprisonment of self-hatred and freed from the shackles of projectionism, perfectionism, moralism/legalism, and unhealthy guilt. Freedom for fidelity demands freedom from enslavement. It is a tired cliché, a battered bumper sticker, an over-used and often superficial slogan, but it is the truth of the gospel: Jesus is the answer.

Glimpse of Jesus

Dear Abba,

I'm starting out free today, free from the advertised lies that promise me everything from four-doors of turbo-charged happiness to some contraption that will shake, rattle, and roll my abs back into a pack I never had even in my twenties. It would be comical if it wasn't so sad: all of our desires to make ourselves worthy of this world but unfit for the world to come. I want to be a follower of the sacred dream, and one day arrive fully free, free at last.

"Now there were some present at that time who told Jesus
about the Galileans whose blood Pilate had mixed with their
sacrifices. Jesus answered, 'Do you think that these Galileans
were worse sinners than all the other Galileans because they
suffered this way? I tell you, no! But unless you repent, you
too will all perish. Or those eighteen who died when the
tower in Siloam fell on them — do you think they were more
guilty than all the others living in Jerusalem? I tell you, no!
But unless you repent, you too will all perish.'"

LUKE 13:1-5

The Christian living out of the center stares long and compas-
sionately at the skeletal bodies of Ethiopian children, the de-
mented locked up in insane asylums, the addicts on Skid Row,
the children with Down's syndrome, and attempts neither to
justify God's silence nor to get Him off the hook by lamely
explaining why bad things happen to good people, or point-
ing to the randomness of the universe, or anything else. The
God of Jesus Christ is God, Lord and Ruler, and the Christian
surrenders with boundless confidence because God is also
Father. Don't try to understand it. You won't succeed. Don't
try to see it. You can't. Try to live it, and you will be living out
of the center.

The Relentless Tenderness of Jesus

Dear Abba,

I must be honest: it is a frightening surrender. There is so much, too much, that I
cannot square with Your love and mercy.
The suffering and pain are matters too great
for me. And so like the infant who finally
stops squirming and whimpering and gives
in to the parental embrace, I give up and
give in because I've given out. I want to live
tomorrow out of the center, but for now, for
this night, let me rest in Your eyes, in the
center of the storm of perfect love. This I
boldly ask.

"Which of you fathers, if your son asks for a fish, will give him a snake instead? Or if he asks for an egg, will give him a scorpion? If you then, though you are evil, know how to give good gifts to your children, how much more will your Father in heaven give the Holy Spirit to those who ask him!"

LUKE 11:11-13

Perhaps the main reason that we are such poor practitioners of the art of being human; why we so often teeter on a tight-rope between self-hatred and despair is that we don't pray. We pray so little, so rarely, and so poorly. For everything else we have adequate leisure time. Visits, get-togethers, movies, foot-ball games, concerts, an evening with friends, an invitation we can't decline — and these are good because it is natural and wholesome that we come together in community. But when God lays claim on our time, we balk. Do we really believe that He delights to talk with His children? If God had a face, what kind of face would He make at you right now?

Souvenirs of Solitude

Dear Abba,

The face You are making at me right now is
not a scorpion-snake face. It's not even an
egg-fish face. Your face is radiant with ice-
cream-cone delight that I am talking with
You, lingering with You, listening to You,
just spending time with You. Send the good
gift of Your Spirit this day, I pray; come and
be ever near. Forgive my fearful distance
and my distracted mind. Yes, yes, I know.
You have always loved me and always will.
You are such a good Father.

"When he had finished washing their feet, he put on his
clothes and returned to his place. 'Do you understand what
I have done for you?' he asked them. 'You call me "Teacher"
and "Lord," and rightly so, for that is what I am. Now that
I, your Lord and Teacher, have washed your feet, you also
should wash one another's feet.'"

JOHN 13:12-14

The power games we play, whether gross or subtle, are di-
rected toward dominating people and situations, thereby
increasing our prestige, influence, and reputation. Our myriad
methods of manipulation, control, and passive aggression create a life that is little more than a series of competitive moves
and countermoves. We have convinced ourselves that we
must have power in order to be happy. We have developed a
fine radar system attuned to the actions and vibrations of any
person or situation that even remotely threatens our position
of authority. Our ineffectiveness in developing deeply loving
relationships — with others as well as with God — is rooted
in our power addiction.

The Importance of Being Foolish

Dear Abba,

I increased my social standing today, en-
hanced my platform, extended my reach
into the lives of yesterday's strangers, and
made them today's friends. I feel pretty
good about things and then there You are,
standing with a towel and basin asking if
You can wash my feet. And I realize the dust
on my soul is not dust at all but rather the
dirt and sweat and grime of private ambi-
tion caked-on from trying to build my own
kingdom this day. Wash not just my feet,
Lord, but all of me. Wash me clean from the
throne-games that have absolutely nothing
to do with Your kingdom coming and Your
will being done.

"When Jesus came to the region of Caesarea Philippi, he asked his disciples, 'Who do people say the Son of Man is?' They replied, 'Some say John the Baptist; others say Elijah; and still others, Jeremiah or one of the prophets.' 'But what about you?' he asked. 'Who do you say I am?' Simon Peter answered, 'You are the Messiah, the Son of the living God.'"

MATTHEW 16:13-16

Jesus Christ is the Son of God and the Son of Man, the Son of David and the Son of Mary. He is the Word-made-flesh, the Incarnation of the compassion of the Father. He is Messiah, Savior, Dreamer and Storyteller, Servant, Friend, and Parable of God. Close to the brokenhearted, He speaks words of comfort; He revives the crushed in spirit with words of consolation. Rescuing drunks, scalawags, and ragamuffins, He is the Shepherd who feeds, leads, and searches out. He is Prophet, Poet, and Troublemaker, the Scourge of hypocrites and authority figures who use religion to control others, sending them sagging under great burdens of regulations, watching them stumble and refusing to offer assistance. . . . When He looks out at the bedraggled, beat-up, bollixed, and burnt-out, His heart overflows with unspeakable tenderness.

Above All

Dear Abba,

I too easily become distracted by who *the people* say You are when Your question is infinitely more specific: "Who do *you* say that I am?" I say You are unique — uncreated, infinite, totally other, transcending all human concepts, considerations, and expectations. You are beyond anything I can intellectualize or imagine. But on this morning what seems most clear to me is that You are a scandal, because You love not just *the people* but You love *me:* a sheep prone to wander and a prodigal still in love with the far country. Your love is beyond measure.

"Then Judas (not Judas Iscariot) said, 'But, Lord, why do you intend to show yourself to us and not to the world?' Jesus replied, 'Anyone who loves me will obey my teaching. My Father will love them, and we will come to them and make our home with them. Anyone who does not love me will not obey my teaching. These words you hear are not my own; they belong to the Father who sent me. All this I have spoken while still with you.'"

JOHN 14:22-25

Home is that sacred place — external or internal — where we don't have to be afraid; where we are confident of hospitality and love. In our society we have many homeless people sleeping not only on the streets, in shelters or in welfare hotels, but vagabonds who are in flight, who never come home to themselves. They seek a safe place through alcohol or drugs, or security in success, competence, friends, pleasure, notoriety, knowledge, or even a little religion. They have become strangers to themselves, people who have an address but are never at home, who never hear the voice of love or experience the freedom of God's children.

The Ragamuffin Gospel

Dear Abba,

I passed them right and left today: homeless vagabonds who are strangers to
themselves. Then as I passed a storefront
I caught a glimpse of myself, and realized
I am one too. I have an address but I'm
not at home. I'm a man in flight afraid to
turn around lest I run into myself. So I'm
clinging to Your words this evening: "You
have a home . . . I am your home . . . claim
Me as your home . . . you will find it to be
the intimate place where I have found My
home . . . it is right where you are . . . in your
innermost being . . . in your heart." I don't
want to be afraid any longer.

"This is how love is made complete among us so that we will have confidence on the day of judgment: In this world we are like Jesus. There is no fear in love. But perfect love drives out fear, because fear has to do with punishment. The one who fears is not made perfect in love."

1 JOHN 4:17-18

While we profess our faith in God's unconditional love, many of us still live in fear. Nouwen remarks: "Look at the many 'if' questions we raise: What am I going to do if I do not find a spouse, a house, a job, a friend, a benefactor? What am I going to do if they fire me, if I get sick, if an accident happens, if I lose my friends, if my marriage does not work out, if a war breaks out? What if tomorrow the weather is bad, the buses are on strike, or an earthquake happens? What if someone steals my money, breaks into my house, rapes my daughter, or kills me?" Once these questions guide our lives, we take out a second mortgage in the house of fear.

The Ragamuffin Gospel

Dear Abba,

Rather than a life of faith I seem to be living a life of contingencies. Rather than an open-armed *yes!* I've got an anxious brow and nervous hands and a mouthful of *what ifs?* I truly am a prodigal, demanding my cake and eating it too when all I really want to do is go home to that safe place where I don't have to be afraid, where everything is freedom and light and love. I want to experience the glorious liberty of a child of God. And so this day I will not ask *what if?* but rather *why not? Yes, why not!*

"What good is it, my brothers and sisters, if someone claims
to have faith but has no deeds? Can such faith save them?
Suppose a brother or a sister is without clothes and daily
food. If one of you says to them, 'Go in peace; keep warm and
well fed,' but does nothing about their physical needs, what
good is it? In the same way, faith by itself, if it is not accompa-
nied by action, is dead."

                                                          JAMES 2:14-17

Substituting theoretical concepts for acts of love keeps life
at a safe distance. This is the dark side of putting *being* over
doing. Is this not the accusation that Jesus leveled against
the religious elite of His day? The Christian commitment is
not an abstraction. It is a concrete, visible, courageous, and
formidable way of being in the world, forged by daily choices
consistent with inner truth. A commitment that is not visible
in humble service, suffering discipleship, and creative love is
an illusion. Jesus Christ is impatient with illusions, and the
world has no interest in abstractions. "Everyone who listens
to these words of mine and does not act on them will be like
a stupid man who built his house on sand" (Matt. 7:26 JB).
If we bypass these words of the Great Rabbi, the spiritual life
will be nothing more than a fantasy.

                                                          Abba's Child

Dear Abba,

Far worse than men behaving badly is
Christians behaving stupidly. I want to act,
not rashly or blindly — charging every hill
— but consistently with heart-felt compassion for the hungry and the homeless
and the naked and the prisoner. In such
action I feed You and shelter You and clothe
You and visit You. Today I was more goat
than sheep. But in the hope of tomorrow's
mercy, I commit to a courageous way of
being not just *on* the world, but *in* it.

"For I am convinced that neither death nor life, neither angels nor demons, neither the present nor the future, nor any powers, neither height nor depth, nor anything else in all creation, will be able to separate us from the love of God that is in Christ Jesus our Lord."

ROMANS 8:38-39

Jesus Who lives for those in whom love is dead, and Who died that His killers might live, reveals a Father Who has no wrath. The Father cannot be offended, nor can He be pleased by what people do. This is the very opposite of indifference. The Lord does not cherish us as we deserve — if that were the case, we would be desolate — but as He must, unable to do otherwise. He is love. Hard as it is for us to believe — because we neither give nor receive love among ourselves in this way — we yet believe, because of the life-death-resurrection of the Carpenter-Messiah, that His Father is more loving, more forgiving, more cherishing than Abraham, Isaac, or Jacob could have dreamed. What this says simply is that the God and Father of our Lord Jesus Christ is gracious. His love is gratuitous in a way that defies our imagination.

Lion & Lamb

Dear Abba,

Knee-deep in my favorite sins I believed
there was a limit, a threshold to Your love, a
point at which You would say "enough." But
as the dawn shatters the night sky, Your love
has continually shattered that belief; You
are more than my dreams; Your mercies
are new each day; Your compassions fail
not. And so I draw in breath convinced and
humbled, and yet at the same time I trem-
ble because Your love is gratuitous; You are
too much.

"Why, my soul, are you downcast? Why so disturbed within me? Put your hope in God, for I will yet praise him, my Savior and my God."

PSALM 42:5

"The devil never rejoices more," said Francis of Assisi, "than when he robs a servant of God of his peace of heart." Peace and joy go a-begging when the heart of a Christian pants for one sign after another of God's merciful love. Nothing is taken for granted, and nothing is received with gratitude. The troubled eyes and furrowed brow of the anxious believer are the symptoms of a heart where trust has not found a home. The Lord himself must pass through all the shades of the emotional spectrum with us — from rage to tears to amusement. But the poignant truth remains: we do not trust Him. We do not have the mind of Christ.

Gentle Revolutionaries

Dear Abba,

I feel like the psalmist tonight — downcast.
I was upcast, bright, enjoying the warmth
of the day and then suddenly my joy was
pickpocketed. It was a small thing, a minor
misunderstanding that I could have let roll
off like water, but I held on to it and nursed
it a while, and like sin always does, it grew.
Now I find my mind completely disturbed,
anxious, angry, and my imagination is con-
juring up all sorts of somebody-done-me-
wrong songs. Why do I not trust You? After
so many demonstrations of Your infinitely
tender hand, why do I not trust You?

"Or haven't you read in the Law that the priests on Sabbath duty in the temple desecrate the Sabbath and yet are innocent? I tell you that something greater than the temple is here. If you had known what these words mean, 'I desire mercy, not sacrifice,' you would not have condemned the innocent. For the Son of Man is Lord of the Sabbath."

MATTHEW 12:5-8

Several years ago when the Friday abstinence was still in force, a beleaguered fan approached me in Yankee Stadium. It was a Friday. "I had a long day, Father. Not even time for lunch. Worked overtime tonight. I was wondering if I could get a hot dog?" Mentally, I thumbed through my moral theology manual for mitigating circumstances: nuclear holocaust, famine, lunar attack, wedding anniversary. . . . What would Jesus have said? "Bring two!"

Prophets and Lovers

Dear Abba,

Help me remember this day that there is
always something greater than a moralism
going on. It's tempting to reduce things
to that denominator, but I've witnessed
too many times that the math never works
and the innocent are usually cast in a less-
than-flattering light. You desire mercy, not
sacrifice. Period. You are the Lord of the
Sabbath, and the Lord of hot dogs, and the
Lord of me.

"If we confess our sins, he is faithful and just and will forgive us our sins and purify us from all unrighteousness. If we claim we have not sinned, we make him out to be a liar and his word is not in us."

1 JOHN 1:9-10

The Crucified says, "Confess your sin so that I may reveal Myself to you as Lover, Teacher, and Friend, that fear may depart and your heart can stir once again with passion." His word is addressed both to those filled with a sense of self-importance and to those crushed with a sense of self-worthlessness. Both are preoccupied with themselves. Both claim a godlike status, because their full attention is riveted either on their prominence or their insignificance. They are isolated and alienated in their self-absorption. The release from chronic egocentricity starts with letting Christ love them where they are.

Abba's Child

Dear Abba,

Self-importance? Self-worthlessness?
I've covered both bases today. In fact, I've
rounded them several times, and yes, they
both have everything to do with me and
nothing to do with You. I confess to You,
Crucified One, that I've grown really tired
of myself. Like a sponge that's reached its
limit, I've absorbed too much of myself; I
can't take any more. Yet here in this bog of
isolated alienation, You love me. Give me
strength to let You love me. I really can't
take any more of myself.

Thirteenth Day   *Morning*

"Bless those who curse you, pray for those who mistreat you.
If someone slaps you on one cheek, turn to them the other
also. If someone takes your coat, do not withhold your shirt
from them. Give to everyone who asks you, and if anyone
takes what belongs to you, do not demand it back."

LUKE 6:28-30

The Christian response to evil — to aggression — is resistance, of course, but nonviolent resistance, the resistance of
love, prayer, and accepted suffering. When Christians do anything else, they have parted company with Jesus. Nonviolence
is the expression of a faith that the greatest Power in human
history is the forward movement of love. Nonviolence is as realistic as Jesus Himself, and it is one with the cross of Christ's
victory over evil. The question of whether or not nonviolent
resistance "works" should be referred not so much to the gain
of an immediate victory as to the transformation of history
from within by the converging forces of love.

The Relentless Tenderness of Jesus

Dear Abba,

This morning I'm reminded of Foucauld's words: "Not by his words or his works, not even by his miracles, but by his Cross." If my life is to be Christ-like, then it stands my life must be Cross-like. Accepted suffering is not just a good way of doing things, or an ideal to be carried out when convenient — it's the only way to overcome evil. The only way. This goes cross-grain to every molecule in me, Father. Yet I pray not my will this day, but Yours. I am poor and needy, so come to me speedily. And help me take it like a Christian.

"Jesus replied: " 'Love the Lord your God with all your heart
and with all your soul and with all your mind.' This is the first
and greatest commandment. And the second is like it: 'Love
your neighbor as yourself.' All the Law and the Prophets hang
on these two commandments."

MATTHEW 22:37-40

The Jesus-and-me mindset tells us that all we have to do is
accept Christ as Savior, read the Bible, go to church, and save
our souls. Christianity becomes simply a telephone booth
affair, a private conversation between God and me without
reference to my brothers and sisters. I go to church on Sunday while the world goes to hell. When preoccupation with
my personal salvation drugs me into such insensitivity that I
no longer hear the bleating of lost sheep, then Karl Marx was
right: Religion is the opium of the people.

The Signature of Jesus

Dear Abba,

You did not call us into an isolated salvation but one knee-deep in community, shot
straight through with men and women and
children of the ragamuffin variety. Your
magnificent saving plan is not just about
me or even me and my closest friends,
but rather about the whole of humanity,
even creation itself that groans day by day.
When being a Christian individual slips
into Christian individualism then I know
without a shadow of a doubt that while the
outside of my cup may sparkle and shine,
the inside is floating with a dead faith's
bones.

Fourteenth Day *Morning*

"Why do you look at the speck of sawdust in your brother's eye and pay no attention to the plank in your own eye? How can you say to your brother, 'Let me take the speck out of your eye,' when all the time there is a plank in your own eye? You hypocrite, first take the plank out of your own eye, and then you will see clearly to remove the speck from your brother's eye."

MATTHEW 7:3-5

Usually we see other people not as they are, but as we are. A person, in a real sense, is what he or she sees. And seeing depends on our eyes. Jesus uses the metaphor of eyes more often than that of minds or wills. The old proverb, "The eyes are the windows of the soul," contains a profound truth. Our eyes reveal whether our souls are spacious or cramped, hospitable or critical, compassionate or judgmental. The way we see other people is usually the way we see ourselves. If we have made peace with our flawed humanity and embraced our ragamuffin identity, we are able to tolerate in others what was previously unacceptable in ourselves.

The Ragamuffin Gospel

Dear Abba,

I've got spiritual astigmatism, had it for
years. But You know that. Things just get
blurry when I try to focus and I end up
seeing others in error — sometimes slight,
but other times monumental. And yes, that
same vision problem applies to my life. I
often see myself as a severe disappointment
to You and those around me. Create in me
clean eyes, O God, and create a right seeing
within me. Restore to me the clarity of Your
vision and grant me an accepting spirit so
that I may love my brother and sister, and
also myself.

"Therefore, since we have a great high priest who has ascended into heaven, Jesus the Son of God, let us hold firmly to the faith we profess. For we do not have a high priest who is unable to empathize with our weaknesses, but we have one who has been tempted in every way, just as we are — yet he did not sin. Let us then approach God's throne of grace with confidence, so that we may receive mercy and find grace to help us in our time of need."

HEBREWS 4:14-16

Here was a man, Hebrews says, "tempted as we are, yet without sinning" (4:15). Sin does not magnify the suffering of man's plight; instead, it mitigates it. When I sin, I seek an escape from my humanity. I used to say to myself, "Well, you're only human!" But sin does not make me human; it compromises my humanity. The philandering husband with his mistress on business trips, the chemically addicted, the thieves who build ivory towers out of stolen money, the sensation-seekers and power brokers who seek substitutes. They do not drink the poverty of the human situation down to the last drop. They dare not stare it full in the face.

Souvenirs of Solitude

Dear Abba,

Yet. Those three letters stop me in my rutted tracks of besetting sins. For You were tempted as I am, *yet* You did not sin. The humbling point is that on a scale from 1 to 10, I usually give in when the heat reaches 3 or 4, *yet* You experienced the 10 — the full-in-the-face of temptation — and did not give in. You are the friend of sinners, *yet* You are also the Great High Priest who invites us to come with confidence to Your throne and receive both our daily bread and extra rations for emergencies. I sometimes feel I am beginning to understand the depths of Your love, *yet* You continually amaze me.

"The Lord will deliver them to you, and you must do to them all that I have commanded you. Be strong and courageous. Do not be afraid or terrified because of them, for the Lord your God goes with you; he will never leave you nor forsake you."

DEUTERONOMY 31:5-6

I cannot free myself. I must be set free. Yes, the untrammeled freedom of Jesus disturbs me, His utter indifference to human respect makes me uncomfortable, but He invites me to make friends with my insecurities, smile at them, outgrow them in patient endurance, live with the serene confidence that He never abandons His friends even when we disappoint Him, and look forward in expectant faith to the day when I can say to the angry chairperson of the Inscrutable Noonies Society, whose speaking invitation I have just refused, "Frankly, my dear, I don't give a damn!"

A Glimpse of Jesus

Dear Abba,

You have set me free, but I want to be free indeed, free at last. Like a dog that returns to its vomit, I crawl back daily to the prison of respect, to a reliance on the approval of others to keep my spirits high and happy, and each time I realize what a fool I am. Their praise or rejection of me rises and falls like waves on the ocean. Thank You for not abandoning me. Thank You for not berating me for my addiction to chains. Thank You for loving me and constantly standing beyond prison walls, calling me to You, saying, "Come out and play. Life's more fun out here with Me!"

"But now apart from the law the righteousness of God has been made known, to which the Law and the Prophets testify. This righteousness is given through faith in Jesus Christ to all who believe. There is no difference between Jew and Gentile, for all have sinned and fall short of the glory of God, and all are justified freely by his grace through the redemption that came by Christ Jesus."

ROMANS 3:21-24

"Justification by grace though faith" is the theologian's learned phrase for what Chesterton once called "the furious love of God." He is not moody or capricious; He knows no seasons of change. He has a single relentless stance toward us: He loves us. He is the only God man has ever heard of Who loves sinners. False gods — the gods of human manufacturing — despise sinners, but the Father of Jesus loves all, no matter what they do. But of course this is almost too incredible for us to accept. Nevertheless, the central affirmation of the Reformation stands: through no merit of ours, but by His mercy, we have been restored to a right relationship with God through the life, death, and resurrection of His beloved Son. This is the Good News, the gospel of grace.

The Ragamuffin Gospel

Dear Abba,

As I grew older I thought this truth would become easier to accept, but I was wrong. It was, is, and I bet always will simply be too good to be true. That You would love us, all of us, no matter what we've done? Amazing truth! That Your consistent stance toward us, all of us, would be one of furious love? Incredible statement! That because of Your mercy, our wrongs, all of them, have been righted? Staggering insight! That I have been accepted by the gospel of grace? Good news! Very good news!

"Then God said, 'Let us make mankind in our image, in our likeness, so that they may rule over the fish in the sea and the birds in the sky, over the livestock and all the wild animals, and over all the creatures that move along the ground.' So God created mankind in his own image, in the image of God he created them; male and female he created them."

GENESIS 1:26-27

Pain, inconvenience, sin — these are the *problems* of being, the alarming, embarrassing, even tragic things that God is apparently willing to put up with in order to have beings at all. But whatever the problems are, they are not the root of being. That root is *joy* and now. It is important to recapture the *element of delight* in creation. Imagine the ecstasy, the veritable orgy of joy, wonder, and delight when God makes a person in His own image — when God made you. The Father gave you as a gift to Himself. You are a response to the vast delight of God. Out of an infinite number of possibilities, God invested you with existence. Regardless of the mess you may have made out of the original clay, wouldn't you agree with Aquinas that "it is better to be than not to be?"

Souvenirs of Solitude

Dear Abba,

Sometimes I get so entangled in the problems of being that I forget the root, and I miss the forests *and* the trees, not to mention myself. Wipe the sleep from my eyes this morning, Lord, and help me wake up to the truth that I am a response to Your vast delight. Thank You for making me *me*. Thank You for making me in Your image. Restore to me the joy of my existence.

" 'For my thoughts are not your thoughts, neither are your
ways my ways,' declares the Lord. 'As the heavens are higher
than the earth, so are my ways higher than your ways and my
thoughts than your thoughts.' "

ISAIAH 55:8-9

Christian history offers ample testimony that we have con-
trived a god who resembles ourselves, a mirror image of
appetite, fanaticism, financial profit, political muscle, blood-
line, nationality, or whatever our passing fancy, and we have
worshiped this god of human manufacturing, a god who does
not exist. Likewise, the god whose moods alternate between
graciousness and fierce anger, the god who is tender when
we are good and relentlessly punishing when we are bad, the
god who exacts the last drop of blood from his Son so that
his just anger, evoked by sin, may be appeased, is not the God
revealed by and in Jesus Christ. And if he is not the God of
Jesus, he does not exist.

Above All

Dear Abba,

I was guilty of this today, this creating You
in my own image. And so you were a god
today who was impatient with the aged
who long for the good old days; a god who
said black just because the other person
said white; a god who likes the looks of
himself in the mirror; a god who swallows
camels left and right while struggling with
a single gnat. What I created today was a
god, but it was not You. Forgive this sin of
mine, I pray.

"This, then, is how you should pray: 'Our Father in heaven, hallowed be your name, your kingdom come, your will be done, on earth as it is in heaven. Give us today our daily bread. And forgive us our debts, as we also have forgiven our debtors. And lead us not into temptation, but deliver us from the evil one.'"

MATTHEW 6:9-13

Many Christians never have grabbed ahold of God. They do not know, really know, that God dearly and passionately loves them. Many accept it theoretically; others in a shadowy sort of way. While their belief system is invulnerable, their faith in God's love for them is remote and abstract. They would be hard-pressed to say that the essence of their faith-commitment is a love affair between God and themselves. Not just a *simple* love affair but a *furious* love affair. How do we grab ahold of God? . . . The answer comes irresistibly and unmistakably: prayer.

The Signature of Jesus

Dear Abba,

Give us this day our daily bread. But man
does not live by bread alone, so also give us
this day Your other bread, Your provision
of tender mercies that we may take and eat,
for then we can run and walk and sing and
dance and truly not grow weary. You have
taught us the simple prayer; now teach us
the fury of Your kingdom and Your will, on
earth as it is in heaven.

"And if Christ has not been raised, your faith is futile; you are still in your sins. Then those also who have fallen asleep in Christ are lost. If only for this life we have hope in Christ, we are of all people most to be pitied."

I CORINTHIANS 15:17-19

This *yes* is an act of faith, a decisive, wholehearted response of my whole being to the risen Jesus present beside me, before me, around me, and within me; a cry of confidence that my faith in Jesus provides security not only in the face of death but in the face of a worse threat posed by my own malice; a word that must be said not just once but repeated over and over again in the ever-changing landscape of life. An awareness of the resurrected Christ banishes meaninglessness — the dreaded sense that all our life experiences are disconnected and useless — helps us to see our lives as all of one piece, and reveals a design never perceived before.

Abba's Child

Dear Abba,

Now I lay me down to sleep. If I should die before I wake I want my last word in this vale of tears to be *yes*. With my whole being I shout *yes* to Your present risenness; it has been my strength for this day and it is the hope that I shall dream of as I sleep. I say *yes* to Your steadfast love which does not slumber nor sleep and knows no shadow of turning. And I whisper *yes* to the dynamic power of Your gospel, the power to not only keep my soul, but to save my life, and if it be Your will, to wake me tomorrow to a world filled with fresh mercies.

"Be careful not to practice your righteousness in front of
others to be seen by them. If you do, you will have no reward
from your Father in heaven. So when you give to the needy,
do not announce it with trumpets, as the hypocrites do in the
synagogues and on the streets, to be honored by others. Truly
I tell you, they have received their reward in full."

MATTHEW 6:1-2

Jesus says in effect: Like a little child, consider yourself to be
of little account. Blessed are you if you love to be unknown
and regarded as nothing: all things being equal, to prefer
contempt to honor, to prefer ridicule to praise, to prefer
humiliation to glory. To practice poverty of spirit calls us not
to take offense or be supersensitive to criticism. The majority
of hurts in our lives, the endless massaging of the latest bruise
to our wounded ego, feelings of anger, grudges, resentment,
and bitterness come from our refusal to embrace our abject
poverty, from our obsession with our rights, from our need
for esteem in the eyes of others. If I follow the counsel of Jesus
and take the last place, I won't be shocked when others put
me there, too.

Lion & Lamb

Dear Abba,

You know me all too well. I seek out honor
and praise and glory on a daily basis like a
bloodhound. I find it and I'm satisfied, but
only for a day or two as someone or something comes along and ruins it. Then I'm off
again, sniffing out something to prove to
everyone just how spectacular I am. But I
was not created to be a bloodhound, led by
his nose. No, You created me as Your child,
to be led by Your hand, the hand of a loving
Father Who will provide all my needs if I
will just trust You. And Lord, that's where it
gets hard.

"But seek first his kingdom and his righteousness, and all these things will be given to you as well. Therefore do not worry about tomorrow, for tomorrow will worry about itself. Each day has enough trouble of its own."

MATTHEW 6:33-34

"The emotional state of surrender," writes Dr. Harry S. Tiebout, "is a state in which there is a persisting capacity to accept reality. It is a state that is really positive and creative." When the Christian surrenders to the Spirit on the unconscious level, there is no residual battle, and relaxation ensues with freedom from strain and conflict. Submission, on the other hand, is halfhearted acceptance. It is described by such words as *resignation, compliance, acknowledgment, concession,* and so forth. There remains a feeling of reservation, a tug in the direction of non-acceptance. Surrender produces wholehearted acceptance.

The Gentle Revolutionaries

Dear Abba,

My temptation right now is to worry about tomorrow. But tomorrow will worry about itself, won't it? In fact, worrying about *what's to come* dilutes the experience of *what's right now* and leaves me half missing instead of wholly here. Or even holy here. I've no desire to be compliant, but I do want to surrender to Your hand, to give myself wholeheartedly to this moment and this breath and this reality. The now is *this*, tomorrow is *that*. Forgive me for wanting more of *that* than *this*.

"Come to me, all you who are weary and burdened, and I will give you rest. Take my yoke upon you and learn from me, for I am gentle and humble in heart, and you will find rest for your souls. For my yoke is easy and my burden is light."

MATTHEW 11:28-30

The school of humiliation is a great learning experience; there is no other like it. When the gift of a humble heart is granted, we are more accepting of ourselves and less critical of others. Self-knowledge brings a humble and realistic awareness of our limitations. It leads us to be patient and compassionate with others, whereas before we were demanding, insensitive, and stuck-up. Gone are the complacency and narrow-mindedness that made God superfluous. For the humble person there is a constant awareness of his or her own weakness, insufficiency, and desperate need for God.

The Signature of Jesus

Dear Abba,

The common understanding of being unequally yoked is that of a believer being married to an unbeliever. But I've come to see there's more to it than that. I'm unequally yoked when I live my days in smug self-assurance, bloated self-dependence, and nauseating self-confidence. The result is always burdensome, the polar opposite of words like *light* and *easy*. A little self-knowledge goes a long way, doesn't it, Jesus? Being yoked to You, the One gentle and humble in heart, is my only hope of finding rest for my soul, not to mention making me someone others can stand to be around.

"Get rid of all bitterness, rage and anger, brawling and slander, along with every form of malice. Be kind and compassionate to one another, forgiving each other, just as in Christ God forgave you."

EPHESIANS 4:31-32

In returning to ourselves, in contemplating the compassion of Jesus and realizing that "This means me," we come under the Mercy and qualify for the nametag "blessed." In urging us to compassionate caring for others, Jesus invites us to have compassion for ourselves. The measure of our compassion for others lies in proportion to our capacity for self-acceptance and self-affirmation. When the compassion of Christ is interiorized and appropriated to self, the breakthrough into being for others occurs. In a win-win situation, the way of compassionate caring for others brings healing to ourselves, and compassionate caring for ourselves brings healing to others.

A Glimpse of Jesus

Dear Abba,

The inability to be kind and compassionate to myself sets up a lose-lose scenario. I lose the full view of Your mercy for me, and when that's the case, others get a screwball form of mercy from me. Just because I look compassionate and sound compassionate doesn't mean I'm compassionate. Ugh. Rid me of that posing, help me return to myself and realize the depths of Your forgiveness of me, for only then can I truly extend something to others which is life-giving, something which is indeed *good news.*

"For I do not do the good I want to do, but the evil I do not want to do — this I keep on doing. Now if I do what I do not want to do, it is no longer I who do it, but it is sin living in me that does it."

ROMANS 7:19-20

I've been asked a certain question countless times over the course of my ministry. Sometimes it has been asked with genuine sincerity; other times it was a loaded pharisaical grenade: "Brennan, how could you relapse into alcoholism after your Abba encounters?" Here is the response I gave in *The Ragamuffin Gospel* in 1990: It is possible because I got battered and bruised by loneliness and failure; because I got discouraged, uncertain, guilt-ridden, and took my eyes off Jesus. Because the Christ-encounter did not transfigure me into an angel. Because justification by grace through faith means I have been set in a right relationship with God, not made the equivalent of a patient etherized on a table.

All Is Grace

Dear Abba,

Sometimes I wish my encounter with You would have transfigured me into an angel. It sure would've saved some heartache, both in my life and in the lives of those who love me. But the reality is I'm no angel, never have been. I am a man, a man You lived, died, and live again for. I am a sheep prone to wander and wonder, yet You always welcome me back into the fold. If I were You, I would've dropped me a long time ago. But I'm not You and You're not me. I slip and fall but You are steadfast. I take my eyes off You but You continue to know my inmost thoughts. I want to do good, Lord, I really do. But I'm not You. Help.

"For God so loved the world that he gave his one and only Son, that whoever believes in him shall not perish but have eternal life. For God did not send his Son into the world to condemn the world, but to save the world through him."

JOHN 3:16-17

Twenty-one years later I stand by what I wrote; those words are as true for me now as they were then and on the day of my mother's funeral. That paragraph from *Ragamuffin Gospel* spoke to many people; they've told me so time after time. I must admit though that from where I sit today the paragraph is a bit much, a little wordy. I believe I can now whittle the lines down to a three word response that incorporates all the truth of a verbose 1990 ragamuffin into a 2011 ragamuffin's preference for brevity. Question: "Brennan, how could you relapse into alcoholism after your Abba encounters?" Answer: "These things happen."

All Is Grace

Dear Abba,

These things happen. They really do. And
while I grieve them and You know I do, I
also know deep within that these things are
some of the very things that have brought
me to my prodigal senses and sent me run-
ning back to You, back to my Father, back
home. So I don't thank You for these things
but I do thank You for this grace that is
greater than the sum of my sins; this mercy
that knows my good-for-nothing name and
still believes in me; and this tenderness that
I've done nothing to deserve but loves me
anyway.

"You, God, are my God, earnestly I seek you; I thirst for you, my whole being longs for you, in a dry and parched land where there is no water. I have seen you in the sanctuary and beheld your power and your glory. Because your love is better than life, my lips will glorify you."

PSALM 63:1-3

Let us suppose it were so ordained that your eternal destiny was to depend on your personal relationship with a spiritual leader you know. Would you not arrange to spend a little more time with that person than you presently do? Wouldn't you strive to prove worthy of his or her friendship? Wouldn't you try assiduously to eliminate all personality traits displeasing to her from your life? When duties and obligations called you away from his presence, wouldn't you be eager to return to him as "the deer pants for streams of water"? And if this person confided to you that he kept a diary of personal memoirs that were the deepest whisperings of his inner self, wouldn't you be anxious not only to read them but to steep yourself in them so that you might know and love him more?

The Signature of Jesus

Dear Abba,

Of all the things I do today I want the one constant to be that I stay close to You and Your Word; not because I have to, but because I want to. Help me this day, Lord, to pray without ceasing. Not with head bowed and eyes closed, but with all my senses alert to Your abiding presence in which I live and move and have my being. I want to love You more, Jesus, because You first loved me.

"He went away a second time and prayed, 'My Father, if it is not possible for this cup to be taken away unless I drink it, may your will be done.' When he came back, he again found them sleeping, because their eyes were heavy. So he left them and went away once more and prayed the third time, saying the same thing."

MATTHEW 26:42-44

Through the help of Father Francis Martin during a scripture course at Loyola in New Orleans, I learned that the only four places in the New Testament where the phrase "Thy will be done" occurs are in the context of *martyrdom*. In Matthew 26:42, Mark 14:36, and Luke 22:42, Jesus is in the Garden of Gethsemane. As He approaches His martyrdom, He prays to His beloved Abba, "Let Your will be done, not mine." Again in Acts 21:13-14, Paul announced that he was ready for martyrdom: "Why are you crying and breaking my heart in this way? For in the name of the Lord Jesus, I am prepared, not only for imprisonment, but for death, in Jerusalem."

Souvenirs of Solitude

Dear Abba,

I say the Our Father every day. The phrase
"Thy will be done" rolls off my tongue
with little or no effort. Yet I see those are
words I cannot diddle with; they are more
than words, they are a vow. I believe the
marriage vows to be important enough but
how many times today did I break this vow
because I went to great lengths to avoid any
hint of martyrdom? If I saw it, I ran scared,
a coward forgetting that the only way the
seed can grow is if it is buried deep beneath
the surface. I will still pray "Thy will be
done" but I may pray it a little slower from
now on. That phrase scares me, Lord.

"For through the law I died to the law so that I might live for God. I have been crucified with Christ and I no longer live, but Christ lives in me. The life I now live in the body, I live by faith in the Son of God, who loved me and gave himself for me."

GALATIANS 2:19-20

Employing adjectives such as *furious, passionate, vehement,* and *aching* to describe the longing of God are my mumbling and fumbling to express the Inexpressible. Yet, I plod on. Both theology, which is faith seeking understanding, and spirituality, which is the faith-experience of what we understand intellectually, offer a glimpse into the mystery. Now we see only reflections in a mirror, mere riddles (I Cor. 13:12). But someday, the adjectives will give way to the reality. But then there's also that word Chesterton used: *union.* That's one of the most explosive words in my Christian vocabulary. The daring metaphor of Jesus as bridegroom suggests that the living God seeks more than an intimate relationship with us.

The Furious Longing of God

Dear Abba,

You live in me, so what I do or say or don't do or don't say becomes somehow the acts of You? I've got to confess this is a mind-blower, and frankly halts me in my tracks because I did some things yesterday and said some things yesterday that I'm pretty sure You wouldn't do or say. I am so sorry. In the newness of Your mercies this morning, I step into this day with an awareness that I'm stepping as You, because You are in me and I still have a hard time grasping that one, but I pray my steps and my words and everything about me would honor the union we have.

"In all this you greatly rejoice, though now for a little while you may have had to suffer grief in all kinds of trials. These have come so that the proven genuineness of your faith — of greater worth than gold, which perishes even though refined by fire — may result in praise, glory and honor when Jesus Christ is revealed."

1 PETER 1:6-7

Willie Juan sat very quiet. The part of the story about his father always confused him, but the part about his mother made the sorrow come. Every time. "If that would have been the end of the story, it would have been a catastrophe," Calm Sunset said. "But it wasn't. After her funeral I brought you here to live with me. My sweet Willie Juan, you have brought a joy to my days beyond what I ever imagined." "So I'm not a cata . . . catast . . . what did you say?" "Catastrophe. No, you are not, because that would mean your story had no brightness at all. But it does, Willie Juan. I like to say it's a tragedy; that means there is sorrow, but it's also mixed with elements of joy. Only God knows how much I love you, Willie Juan."

Patched Together

Dear Abba,

You were the Man of Sorrows, well ac-
quainted with grief. If the servant is not
above the master, then I too should expect
sorrows and grief. Forgive me when I im-
mediately interpret these things as catastrophe instead of potential. The brightness in
my life is You, Lord. Some days are dark;
in fact, some are pitch-black. But You have
promised that I do not walk alone, that
even the smallest glimmer of light is You
encouraging me farther and farther on.
Thank You that I am not a catastrophe, and
that You love me.

"He has shown you, O mortal, what is good. And what does the Lord require of you? To act justly and to love mercy and to walk humbly with your God."

MICAH 6:8

As we listen to the heartbeat of the Rabbi, we will hear words of reassurance: "I've told you all this beforehand. Shh! Be still. I am here. All is well." In place of end-time agitation and thoughts of doom, Jesus tells us to be alert and watchful. We are to avoid the doomsayer and the talk-show crank when they conduct their solemn televised meeting in the green room of the apocalypse. We are to act justly, to love tenderly, and to walk humbly with our God. We are to claim our belovedness each day and live as servants in the awareness of present risenness. We pay no heed to the quacks and self-proclaimed seers who manipulate the loyalty of others for their self-serving purposes.

Abba's Child

Dear Abba,

I have often been the dumb duck who let the doomsayers lead me on wild pilgrimages filled with panic and anxiety. I have also often been the quack manipulating others for my own sordid gain. Both realities, if they can even be called that, betray my trust in You. It's not a mystery; Your word has it all laid out; I know what to do: behave justly, love compassion, and walk confidently alongside my Abba. Tomorrow's survival is Your responsibility.

"Jesus said to them, 'A prophet is not without honor except in his own town, among his relatives and in his own home.' He could not do any miracles there, except lay his hands on a few sick people and heal them."

MARK 6:4-5

Small wonder that biblical scholar Richard Rohr would say, "The old Baltimore catechism isn't wrong, just inadequate ... it should read: man is made to know how God longs to love and serve him." ... The unflinching, unwavering love and compassion of Jesus Christ, the stranger to self-hatred, is the ultimate source of our healing and wholeness. This was the experience of Jesus' followers. This was the kind of impact He had upon them. This is the real Jesus inscribed on every page of the gospels. If we wish to treat Jesus as our God, we must let Him be who He wants to be for us. Returning to Rohr's observation, we have to conclude that we are made to know how God longs to love and serve us, to free and forgive, to heal and make whole His children.

A Glimpse of Jesus

Dear Abba,

Why is it that here, among Your own people, among those of us that claim to know
You best, that Your mighty works are rare?
Is it because we will not honor You and
allow You to be who You want to be for
us? Something tells me this may be on the
money, maybe not for all of us but I confess
it is for me. It's not that I do not want You
to be that for me, it's that I will not let You
be that for me. I'm sure You marvel at my
unbelief. Help Thou my unbelief.

"He made himself nothing by taking the very nature of a servant, being made in human likeness. And being found in appearance as a man, he humbled himself by becoming obedient to death — even death on a cross!"

PHILIPPIANS 2:7-8

The gospel is absurd and the life of Jesus is meaningless unless we believe that He lived, died, and rose again with but one purpose in mind: to make brand-new creations. Not to make people with better morals, but to create a community of prophets and professional lovers, men and women who would surrender to the mystery of the fire of the Spirit that burns within, who would live in ever greater fidelity to the omnipresent Word of God, who would enter into the center of it all, the very heart and mystery of Christ, into the center of the flame that consumes, purifies, and sets everything aglow with peace, joy, boldness, and extravagant, furious love. This, my friends, is what it really means to be a Christian.

The Furious Longing of God

Dear Abba,

I want to be a Christian in my heart. But
it's my hands that often resist because nails
hurt. And my side pulls away because being
pierced is never enjoyable. And my back
recoils at the mere crack of a whip. And
my forehead is so sensitive to any kind of
thorny object. Surrendering fully to You
means the cross, not Yours but mine, and I
find I am a coward, Lord. But I want to be a
Christian today, I really do.

"Jesus straightened up and asked her, 'Woman, where are they? Has no one condemned you?' 'No one, sir,' she said. 'Then neither do I condemn you,' Jesus declared. 'Go now and leave your life of sin.'"

JOHN 8:10-11

According to Hosea, God is willing to maintain a relationship even when His spouse has become a coarse and vulgar prostitute. This same conviction is carried into the New Testament. The adulterous woman is brought before Jesus. The god of religious leaders, who never got over Hosea's contribution, is expected to judge her. She has been unfaithful and the divine posture embodied in leadership would stone her. The god of the Pharisees is interested in the contract, in justice first and foremost. Let us kill the woman for the contract. The person is expendable. But in the Man, Jesus, we see the human face of God, one in keeping with the Old Testament revelation. He is interested in the woman. His love moves beyond justice and proves more salvific than spelling out the ground rules all over again.

The Ragamuffin Gospel

Dear Abba,

Thank You that You do not deal with me
as my sins deserve. Thank You that on
the last day, when You call my name, You
will say, "Come, Brennan, blessed of my
Father." Thank You that Your invitation to
me on that day will not be because You are
just, but because Your name is Mercy. I've
decided that I may never fully understand
the gospel of Your grace. Then again, understanding is not the goal but acceptance,
right? Either way, thank You. Thank You so
very much.

"I am the vine; you are the branches. If you remain in me and I in you, you will bear much fruit; apart from me you can do nothing. If you do not remain in me, you are like a branch that is thrown away and withers; such branches are picked up, thrown into the fire and burned."

JOHN 15:5-6

I have long been smitten with concepts. They engage my mind, rustle my thought process, and stir my emotions. *Unconditional love* as a concept has transported me to intellectual nirvana, motivated the reading of at least fifty books on related themes, and deluded me into believing that I was *there*. Until along came a day when I was appalled to discover that nothing had changed. It was all a head trip. Lofty thoughts and impersonal concepts left my lousy self-image intact and my way of praying unchanged. Until the love of God that knows no boundary, limit, or breaking point is internalized through personal decision; until the furious longing of God seizes the imagination; until the heart is conjoined to the mind through sheer grace, nothing happens.

The Furious Longing of God

Dear Abba,

Like a pig that returns to its slop, I return to
my head trips, falling in love all over again
with concepts. They are a hard habit to
break because they always almost convince
me I am *there.* But I'm not; I'm *here,* right
here in a recurring scene where my head
is full but my heart is empty. So, like last
time, I'm asking You to blow the doors off
my shabby cabin and rip my heart from its
moorings and breathe fresh life into it once
again. Return unto me the joy of my salvation, one more time.

"And this is his command: to believe in the name of his Son, Jesus Christ, and to love one another as he commanded us. The one who keeps God's commands lives in him, and he in them. And this is how we know that he lives in us: We know it by the Spirit he gave us."

1 JOHN 3:23-24

Many preachers today have decided that Jesus' standard for discipleship is inadequate for modern times. The new criterion is orthodoxy of doctrine coupled with the way we interpret the Bible. "Right thinking" is the new norm for determining what a Christian is worth. In these parlous times we do not shrink from splitting up fellowship, local churches, and even denominations over the form of worship, the songs we sing, or the method of interpreting a Bible passage. My friends in Christ, the simple truth is that the Christian Church in America is divided by doctrine, history, and day-to-day living. We have come a long sad journey from the first century, when pagans exclaimed with awe and wonder, "See how these Christians love one another!"

The Signature of Jesus

Dear Abba,

If I speak and even the angels swoon, but I
have not love . . . if I have the gift of story-
telling and bringing men to tears, but I
have not love . . . if I have the faith to rally
mountains of followers for the cause, but I
have not love . . . if I give all my proceeds to
charity, but find no trace of charity within
myself, then I am nothing more than a
noisy nothing, a distraction for those who
would seek to find and know You. There is
faith, hope, and love, but help me to seek
and practice the greatest of these.

Twenty-Sixth Day   *Morning*

"I am the good shepherd; I know my sheep and my sheep
know me — just as the Father knows me and I know the
Father — and I lay down my life for the sheep."

JOHN 10:14-15

His breakthrough into new life on Easter morning unfettered
Him from the space-time limitations of existence in the flesh
and empowered Him to touch not only Nepal, but New
Orleans, not only Matthew and Magdalene, but me. The Lion
of Judah in His present risenness pursues, tracks, and stalks
us here and now. When we cry out with Jeremiah, "Enough
already! Leave me alone in my melancholy," the Shepherd
replies, "I will not leave you alone. You are Mine. I know each
of My sheep by name. You belong to Me. If you think I am
finished with you, if you think I am a small god that you can
keep at a safe distance, I will pounce upon you like a roaring
lion, tear you to pieces, rip you to shreds and break every
bone in your body. Then I will mend you, cradle you in My
arms and kiss you tenderly."

The Relentless Tenderness of Jesus

Dear Abba,

I'm not sure if I have much more left. I've been pounced on, torn up, ripped raw, and now find myself broker than broke. I've given new meaning to the word *prodigal*. I don't have the strength to walk back to You; I don't think I can even crawl. I've gone astray like a sheep that is lost. But I do long for Your salvation. I do remember Your commandments. So search for this lost lamb. Let me live, O Lord, and I will praise You.

Twenty-Sixth Day *Evening*

"It is for freedom that Christ has set us free. Stand firm, then, and do not let yourselves be burdened again by a yoke of slavery. Mark my words! I, Paul, tell you that if you let yourselves be circumcised, Christ will be of no value to you at all."

The inner child is capable of a spontaneous breakthrough of emotions, but the Pharisee within represses them. This is not a question of being an emotional person or a subdued one. This issue is: Do I express or repress my authentic feelings? John Powell once said with sadness that if he had to write an epitaph for his parents' tombstone, it would say, "Here lie two people who never knew one another." His father could never share his feelings, so his mother never got to know him. To open yourself to another person, to stop lying about your loneliness, to stop lying about your fears and hurts, to be open about your affection, and to tell others how much they mean to you — this is the triumph of the child over the Pharisee and the dynamic presence of the Holy Spirit at work.

Souvenirs of Solitude

Dear Abba,

This open and honest sharing of all feelings
has to begin with You, doesn't it? If I can't
be this way with You then there's a slim-to-
none chance of being this way with another.
All right, I've been scared today. There, I
said it. Things are changing around me at
an alarming rate and I've no control over
them, any of them. I thought my life was
going to go *this* way but it went *that* way and
I'm terrified, like a little child. I don't like it,
but that's the truth, Lord. There, I said it.

"But we have this treasure in jars of clay to show that this all-surpassing power is from God and not from us. We are hard pressed on every side, but not crushed; perplexed, but not in despair."

2 CORINTHIANS 4:7-8

Whatever the addiction — be it a smothering relationship, a dysfunctional dependence, or mere laziness — our capacity to be affected by Christ is numbed. Sloth is our refusal to go on the inward journey, a paralysis that results from choosing to protect ourselves from passion. When we are not profoundly affected by the treasure in our grasp, apathy and mediocrity are inevitable. If passion is not to degenerate into nostalgia or sentimentality, it must renew itself at its source. The treasure is Jesus Christ. He is the Kingdom within. As the signature song of the St. Louis Jesuits goes,

We hold a treasure
not made of gold
in earthen vessels
wealth untold.
One treasure only
The Lord, the Christ
In earthen vessels.

Abba's Child

Dear Abba,

It's one thing to discover the treasure. It's quite another to claim it as my own, as that takes determination and effort: in other words, work. I choose the latter this day. I want to work at not dabbling in religion or worldly prestige, as attractive as they may be, for they are just shadows of an unreal world. I want to put my hand to the plow of Your passion, and till new ground, and move forward in the journey.

"You are my friends if you do what I command. I no longer
call you servants, because a servant does not know his master's business. Instead, I have called you friends, for everything that I learned from my Father I have made known to
you. You did not choose me, but I chose you."

JOHN 15:14-16

One day Zacchaeus is in his shop counting his money and
he hears the prophet of Nazareth is passing by. He wants to
get a look, so he runs down the street. Now remember, this is
Zacchaeus, the wee little man. He's so short he can't see over
the shoulders of the taller men, so he climbs up a sycamore
tree. Interesting, isn't it? He went out on a limb for Jesus. Jesus
looks up and says, "Zacchaeus, come down. I want to have
supper in your house today." Now, when an orthodox Jew,
which Jesus was, says "I want to have supper with you," He's
saying, "I want to enter into a friendship with you."

The Furious Longing of God

Dear Abba,

It's not hard for me to accept You as Father and Savior and Lord and Master. But when it comes to Friend, it's just not as easy. It oughta be, but it's not. The thought that You would want to spend time with me and dine with me and walk with me and be my Friend? That You, the Lord of Glory, would want to be the guest of me, a sinner? That leaves me a man undone. Simply undone. So I finish this day with that thought being the final one for the day — You, Jesus, want to be my Friend.

Twenty-Eighth Day *Morning*

"For it seems to me that God has put us apostles on display
at the end of the procession, like those condemned to die
in the arena. We have been made a spectacle to the whole
universe, to angels as well as to human beings. We are fools for
Christ. . . ."

1 CORINTHIANS 4:9-10

"That's right. I have a challenge for you. Would you like to
hear it?" "Yes," John said. "Go back and live out your name;
live like the beloved of Abba. Some may ask you, but most
others will simply observe the way you live. Some will call
you crazy, some may even try and silence your voice, but
some will stop and wonder. Your courage in living as Abba's
beloved can give others the strength to do the same. For in
the end only one thing remains — Abba's love. Willie Juan
has known that, but the river is calling his name. John, now it
is your turn. Define yourself as one beloved by God."

Patched Together

Dear Abba,

Today it's my turn, my chance to live like
Your beloved. I know some will call me
crazy; some will call me worse, maybe even
a fool; but maybe some, maybe just one,
will see and stop and wonder *what's up with
that guy?* If that one person asks, then I'm
ready to tell. But if my life this day is just a
singular, silent, observable display of Your
tenderness, then that is enough. It is more
than enough, and today is my turn.

"To some who were confident of their own righteousness and looked down on everyone else, Jesus told this parable: 'Two men went up to the temple to pray, one a Pharisee and the other a tax collector.'"

LUKE 18:9-10

Long prayers and big words do not suit ragamuffins. Their mouthpiece is the tax collector in the temple: "God, be merciful to me, a sinner" (Luke 18:13). The ragamuffin knows that she is the tax collector and that refusing to admit it would make her a Pharisee. Tax collectors, nobodies, vagabonds, tramps of Jesus — ragamuffins laugh at their own vanity for wanting to be noticed and for being unnoticeable. Neither are ragamuffins interested in pretensions to self-sufficiency. They know that any declaration of independence from the kindness of others is sheer folly. A Cajun would never ask, "Would you like a ride over to the city?" Rather, he would urge, "Can I carry you across the river?" The automatic "no" of pharisaic hubris must yield to the spontaneous "yes" of the needy.

The Ragamuffin Gospel

Dear Abba,

I realized today that there is a third character who goes up to the temple to pray: the pharisaic tax collector — a ragamuffin who knows she's a ragamuffin and wants to make sure everyone else knows she's a ragamuffin. So she ends up using her sinner status not to cry out for mercy to You, but rather to seek out the attention of others as one who is real and authentic, when in reality she is nothing more than hubris in thrift-shop fashions. I realized this today because I looked in the mirror. God, be merciful to me.

"Brothers and sisters, I could not address you as people who live by the Spirit but as people who are still worldly — mere infants in Christ. I gave you milk, not solid food, for you were not yet ready for it. Indeed, you are still not ready. You are still worldly."

                                                    1 CORINTHIANS 3:1-3

The obsession with erotica in book, film, play, and entertainment signals entrapment in the sensation center. The carnal man is blatantly in the flesh and lives and walks according to the flesh. Yet many committed Christians who decry the rampant pornography of our sensate culture still dabble discreetly in the fleshpots and paralyze the power of the Spirit in their lives! An ambivalent "prudence of the flesh" seeks a sort of gilded mediocrity where the self is carefully distributed between flesh and spirit with a watchful eye on both. Paul calls these "men of imperfect spiritual vision." They have received the Spirit, but they remain spiritual men in embryo because they do not subject themselves fully to the domination of the Spirit; they yield to sexual passion and other drives, thus confining themselves to an infantile spirituality.

                                                    The Gentle Revolutionaries

Dear Abba,

It's not You, but me. I'm the one who dilutes Your power in my life with my measured yielding to the demands of the flesh. I'm the one who wants to have the very best of both worlds. I'm the one who has been in Your family for years yet I'm still an infant, carnal, worldly. Help me this day to not even have a hint of sexual immorality, impurity, or greed about me. Yes, I know, Lord; it's time to grow up.

"This is the first and greatest commandment. And the second is like it: 'Love your neighbor as yourself.' All the Law and the Prophets hang on these two commandments."

MATTHEW 22:38-40

In order to love our neighbors as ourselves, we must come to recognize our intrinsic worth and dignity and to love ourselves in the wholesome, appreciative way that Jesus commanded when He said, "Love your neighbor as yourself." The tendency to continually berate ourselves for real or imaginary failures, to belittle ourselves and underestimate our worth, to dwell exclusively on our dishonesty, self-centeredness, and lack of personal discipline, is the influence of our negative self-esteem. Reinforced by the critical feedback of our peers and the reproofs and humiliations of our community, we seem radically incapable of accepting, forgiving, or loving ourselves. In his opening address at the regional charismatic conference in Atlantic City, New Jersey, Father Francis McNutt touched an exposed nerve when he said, "If Jesus Christ has forgiven you all your sins and washed you in His own blood, what right do you have not to forgive yourself?"

The Importance of Being Foolish

Dear Abba,

"Are you letting Jesus love you?" I've asked
that question of others for years; it has
become almost a signature phrase for me;
people expect to hear it. But most of them
have no inkling the degree to which that
question has haunted me for years, and
still does today. I was hard on myself today,
I focused on my sins to the exclusion of
Your mercy; my trees overshadowed Your
forest. If You were to stand before me, right
now, and ask, "Are you letting Me love you,
Brennan?" I would have to say, "I'm trying,
Lord. I'm trying."

"My beloved spoke and said to me, 'Arise, my darling, my beautiful one, come with me. See! The winter is past; the rains are over and gone. Flowers appear on the earth; the season of singing has come, the cooing of doves is heard in our land.'"

SONG OF SONGS 2:10-12

The furious longing of God is beyond our wildest desires, our hope or hopelessness, our rectitude or wickedness, neither cornered by sweet talk nor gentle persuasion. The furious longing of God, as Dan Berrigan writes, is "not to be reduced to a thing, a grand ideal; it is not to be reduced to a plaything, a caged songbird, for the amusement of children." It cannot be tamed, boxed, captivated, housebroken, or templebroken. It is simply and startlingly Jesus, the effulgence of the Father's love. The seldom-stated truth is that many of us have a longing for God and an aversion to God. Some of us seek Him and flee Him at the same time. We may scrupulously observe the Ten Commandments and rarely miss church on a Sunday morning, but a love affair with Jesus is just not our cup of tea.

The Furious Longing of God

Dear Abba,

To think that You seek intimacy with me leaves me in shock bordering on disbelief, wonder akin to incredulity, and affectionate awe tinged by doubt. I've used those words over the years and I stand by them; I cannot find others more suitable to describe this daily, dogged pursuit of my heart. Forgive me for playing hard-to-get. And thank You for not giving up on me.

Thirtieth Day *Evening*

"Not so with you. Instead, whoever wants to become great among you must be your servant, and whoever wants to be first must be your slave — just as the Son of Man did not come to be served, but to serve, and to give his life as a ransom for many."

MATTHEW 20:26-28

Ragamuffins don't sit down to be served; they kneel down to serve. When there is food on their plate, they don't whine about the mystery meat or the soggy veggies, nor do they whimper about the monotonous menu or the cracked plate. Glad for a full stomach, they give thanks for the smallest gift. They do not grow impatient and irritable with the dismal service in department stores, because they so often fail to be good servants themselves. Ragamuffins do not complain about the feeble preaching and the lifeless worship of their local church. They are happy to have a place to go where they can mingle with other beggars at the door of God's mercy. "Beggars know how to open their hands," writes Sue Monk Kidd, "trusting that the crumb of grace will fall." Humbly acknowledging that they are proletarian folks powerless to achieve their heart's desires without divine help, they are grateful for the smallest crumb that tumbles from the preacher's mouth.

The Ragamuffin Gospel

Dear Abba,

Today I've whined about everything from
soggy veggies to sorry sermons. I've really
let out the length of the reins, securing
my place in the minds of a few family and
friends as the embodiment of the words
irritable, complaining, and *grumble.* I've
been an absolute bear, Lord. So first of all,
I'm sorry; please forgive me. And secondly,
I'm opening my hands to You, trusting that
the crumbs of Your grace are sufficient for
bears like me.

"If anyone has material possessions and sees a brother or sister in need but has no pity on them, how can the love of God be in that person? Dear children, let us not love with words or speech but with actions and in truth."

1 JOHN 3:17-18

One of the most shocking contradictions in Christian living is the intense dislike many disciples of Jesus have for themselves. They are more displeased, impatient, irritated, unforgiving and spiteful with their own shortcomings than they would ever dream of being with someone else's. They are fed up with themselves, sick of their own mediocrity, disgusted by their own inconsistency, bored by their own monotony. They would never judge any other of God's children with the savage self-condemnation with which they crush themselves. Through experiencing the relentless tenderness of Jesus, we learn first of all to be gentle with ourselves. To the extent that we allow the *splangchnizomai* of the Lord to invade our hearts, we are freed from the dyspepsia toward ourselves that follows us everywhere, that self-hatred that we are now even ashamed of.

Lion and Lamb

Dear Abba,

I want to live this day as a friend to myself. Give me the strength to be pleasantly
surprised with myself instead of displeased,
long-suffering with my shortcomings instead of impatient, and nice-and-easy-going
instead of irritated. Invade my heart, I pray,
with your tenderness so my eyes will be
clear to see my brothers and sisters in their
need. And may I not respond in just word
or speech but mainly in actions and truth,
being a friend to myself and others.

"God is our refuge and strength, an ever-present help in trouble. Therefore we will not fear, though the earth give way and the mountains fall into the heart of the sea, though its waters roar and foam and the mountains quake with their surging."

PSALM 46:1-3

I have said countless times that losing our illusions is difficult because illusions are the stuff we live by. We believe we're invincible until cancer comes knocking, or we believe we're making a comeback until we tumble down the stairs. God strips away those falsehoods because it is better to live naked in truth than clothed in fantasy. The last few years have been a "stripping away" like I've never experienced. About all I'm left with now is rags, somewhat fitting I guess for a man who has preached such a gospel. If I ever was a ragamuffin, I am now. For ragamuffins, God's name is Mercy; or in the present vernacular of my life — *Help.*

All Is Grace

Dear Abba,

If nobody remembers my name or the
works of my hands, if everything that I've
worked so hard to build over the years
crumbles into insignificance, if I lose my
health and my wits and even, heaven forbid,
my memory, You are still my refuge and
strength. Your name is Mercy. You are my
help, and not just mine but the help of all
the ragamuffins in this life. Better is one
day in Your courts, naked in truth, than a
thousand elsewhere in the land of illusions.
Come, Lord Jesus.

Acknowledgments

The author and publisher wish to thank the following for permission to reprint material from the following publications:

Abba's Child: The Cry of the Heart for Intimate Belonging by Brennan Manning. © 1994 by Brennan Manning. Reprinted by permission of NavPress.

Above All by Brennan Manning. © 2003 by Brennan Manning. Reprinted by permission of Integrity Publishers.

All Is Grace: A Ragamuffin Memoir by Brennan Manning. © 2011 by Brennan Manning. Reprinted by permission of David C. Cook.

The Furious Longing of God by Brennan Manning. © 2009 by Brennan Manning. Reprinted by permission of David C. Cook.

A Glimpse of Jesus: The Stranger to Self-Hatred by Brennan Manning. © 2003 by Brennan Manning. Reprinted by permission of HarperCollins Publishers.

The Importance of Being Foolish: How to Think Like Jesus by Brennan